MiNGiN' or Mint?

essential modern english

Tim Collins is originally from Manchester,
but now lives and works in London.
His other books include *School Rules*.

Mingin' OR Blingin'

essential modern english

tim collins

Michael O'Mara Books Limited

First published in Great Britain in 2005 by
Michael O'Mara Books Limited
9 Lion Yard, Tremadoc Road
London SW4 7NQ

A CIP catalogue record for this book is available from the British Library

ISBN 1-84317-163-5

1 3 5 7 9 10 8 6 4 2

www.mombooks.com

Designed and typeset by Envy Design

Printed in Great Britain by William Clowes Ltd, Beccles, Suffolk

Introduction

Over the last few years, spoken English has been replaced by a new language: *Blinglish*.

It's no longer alright to say you 'dislike' something; you have to say it's *minging*. It's no longer acceptable to say you 'like' something; you have to say it's *blazin'*. And if you haven't quite grasped that being called a *chief* isn't a compliment, you can end up in all sorts of trouble.

This new language comes from a variety of sources – from hip-hop speak like *bling* and *crunk*, West Indian words like *ting* and *batty*, *chav* words like *believe* and *result*, regional British words like *tidy* and *buzzin'* and US words like *lame* and *whatever*. The *Blinglish* language is evolving at a pace, and absorbing every possible influence.

It's a language that's constantly shifting. Words change their meaning, or are replaced by new ones, as soon as the mainstream media absorbs them. One thing that is certain about this language, however, is that you'll be a social outcast if you can't understand it. When your friends, colleagues and even your family are speaking *Blinglish*, it's time to find out what they're on about.

Fortunately, if you want to learn *Blinglish*, you've come to the right place. *Mingin' or Blingin'* lists all the essential words that have entered into widespread usage over the last few years. In fact, the terms listed in this book are so *nang*, so *dutty* and so downright *gravy* that the merest glance at them will transform even the saddest *disco vicar* into the most badass *gangsta pimp hustler hardcore mofo playa* in the *hood*.

Tim Collins, 2005

A

aggie

To be aggravated. As in:

'Did you see how aggie Tanya got last night?
She was getting *well menstrual*.'

See also *flexing, vexed*.

air

To get ignored by someone. As in:

'Dave just tried to talk to that girl over there and he got pure air.'

See also *blank, denied*.

AK

**The AK-47 assault rifle, designed by Kalashnikov.
As boasted about by *gangsta* rappers and, less credibly,
by fifteen-year-old boys from Chatham.**

aks

Blinglish for 'ask'. As in:

> 'Will you aks Wayne out for me?'

all that

Superior, at the top of your game. As in:

> 'Just cos you've got the new Nokia
> doesn't mean you're all that, you know.'

all up in my business

Meddling in my affairs. Variations include 'all up in my grill', 'all up in my hair' and 'all up in my shit'.

alpha

A term referring to the head animal in a pack that's now used to intensify an insult. Examples include 'alpha slut', 'alpha nerd' and 'alpha minger'.

> See also *über*.

alright

Someone who meets with the approval of *townies*.
Someone who isn't a *mosher*, a *greb*, or a *freak*. As in:

'Don't batter him, Darren, he's alright.'

and that

Two words that can be added to the end of any sentence, and
contribute no meaning whatsoever. As in:

'I've just been down to Aldi and that.'

See also *innit*, *ting*.

anyways

Simply means 'anyway', but is a good example of the tendency
to gratuitously add the letter 's' to words, as in the song, 'You
Knows I Loves You' by Goldie Lookin' Chain.

aren't you just the man?

The question to ask someone who's boasting about
something unimpressive.

See also *do you want a medal?*

arm candy
An attractive woman accompanying an unattractive but often richer man.

ayo
'Hey you!' To get someone's attention. As in:

'Ayo! Give us a quid and we'll mind your car for you.'

B

baby mother / baby father
The estranged mother or father of your child. As in:

'Hey baby, let's take off the glove tonight.
You can be one of my baby mothers.'

back in the day
The distant past, as remembered fondly. Often used by teenagers to describe a worryingly recent time, like the late nineties and early noughties.

Words With Different Meanings In the US and the UK

WORD	US	UK
bent	high on drugs	homosexual
bird	a fist with the middle finger extended	a woman
bum	a homeless person	someone's backside, or anal sex
fanny	an arse	a pussy
hardcore	rock music	techno music
juiced	drunk	had sex with
jock	an athlete	a Scot
pants	trousers	underpants, or something not very good
pissed	angry	drunk
raw	cool	wrong
tramp	a whore	a homeless person

MiNGiN' an Blingin'

back of the net!

Exclamation of victory popularized by Alan Partridge. As in:

'I've sold over a hundred pounds worth of industrial cleaning equipment today. Back of the net!'

See also *cashback!, get in!, kiss my face!*.

backwash

The little bit of spit that goes into a bottle or can when someone drinks from it. As in:

'Don't share your Fanta with Graham, he'll backwash it.'

bacon

An insulting term for police derived from 'the pigs'. As in:

'I smell bacon.'

bad

A word that famously reversed its meaning in the eighties. Still used in modern *Blinglish*, although it can be substituted with a whole host of others.

See also blazin', bo, gnarly, gravy, heavy, mint, nang, off the hook, phat, rude, safe, shibby, shiznit, sick, tidy, tight.

bad boy

A *gangsta*. Can also be used as an adjective. As in:

'Check out Barry's bad boy sneakers.'

bail

To leave.

See also bounce, chip off, dip out, do one, rock and roll!.

baller

A basketball player, and by association, someone who's escaped from the *hood* to find success and wealth.

See also soldier.

bare

Means 'very' or 'lots of'. As in:

'There was bare *fit* girls in Legends last night.'

See also hella.

13

batty boy

A homosexual man. From the West Indian word 'batty', meaning 'backside'.

batty rider

Perhaps surprisingly, not another patois term for homosexual, but a very skimpy and tight pair of shorts.

beats

Hard punches delivered to the upper arm as punishment for something like flinching or saying the same word at the same time as someone else.

See also hand out some slaps, licks, open a can of whoopass, smack down, spark, tumps.

beef

To have a disagreement with someone. Could be anything from a dangerous and long-running feud between LA gangs to ignoring your best friend because he stole an orange Club from your lunchbox.

believe

Chavvy way of agreeing with someone. As in:

Chav 1: These Lidl burgers are just as
quality as the ones in *maccy ds*.

Chav 2: Believe.

benjamins

Money. Derived from US President Benjamin Franklin's appearance on the $100 bill. As in:

'I wanted to get a McFlurry as well, but I didn't have enough benjamins.'

See also *cheddar, cream, dead presidents, dollars, franklins, notes, papers.*

bent

Means drunk or *drug-fucked* in the US, but in the UK refers to someone who's a willie-woofter.

See also Words With Different Meanings In the US and the UK, page 11.

15

bestest

Even better than the best. As in:

'Charmaine is my bestest friend.'

See also *most bestest.*

biffa

A fat or ugly girl. As in:

'Wayne copped off with this right biffa in Volts last night. She looked like a pig in knickers.'

See also *fugly, gipper, gonk, minger, munter, swamp donkey, ug, wouldn't touch her with yours.*

big-massive-no-way-fuck-off

A term emphasizing the size of something, and used primarily in the north-west of Britain. As in:

'Jay's just had this big-massive-no-way-fuck-off spoiler fitted on to his XR3i.'

big time / big style

Two ways of expressing agreement that sound a bit *disco vicar*-ish now. As in:

Office junior: I didn't know you liked R 'n' B.

Team leader: Big time.

big up

To recommend something, or to congratulate someone. Hence, 'bigging yourself up', to gloat or show off.

See also *flexing*, *stunt*.

bingo wings

The flabby skin which hangs down from the upper arms of middle-aged women. Also known as 'nan flaps'.

bitch

- A woman, as pronounced 'beeatch' by *gangstas* and wannabes. Calling someone *your* bitch rather than *a* bitch is not necessarily an insult. As in:

'I think you're *buff*, would you be my bitch?'

17

- **A man who is under his girlfriend's thumb.** As in:

'Why didn't you show up last night? You're turning into Karen's bitch.'

- **Someone on the receiving end in a homosexual relationship.** As in:

'Do you want to go to prison and end up as someone's bitch?'

- **To moan or complain.** As in:

'If you don't stop your bitching I'll have to put the *smack down*.'

- **A spiteful, difficult or dislikeable person, usually a woman.**

bitch slap

A weak slap. Threatening to bitch slap someone implies that a proper, masculine punch will not be required to put them in their place.

bitch tits

Man breasts. Can also be used as a nickname for any overweight male. As in:

'Hey bitch tits! What's your bra size?'

bite

- **British term for stealing or copying something. As in:**

'I was the first one to wear a Hackett shirt with the collar turned up. Wayne and Trevor bit my style.'

- **US word for something regrettable or unfortunate. As in:**

Trailer Trash 1: My mom just got a restraining order put out on my real dad.

Trailer Trash 2: That bites.

blank

To ignore someone, or be ignored by them – especially used in the context of chatting someone up. As in:

Bloke returning to his mates in nightclub: Naah, she wasn't very *fit* close up.

Friends: Blanked!

See also *air*, *denied*.

blazin'

Chavvy word for something that is excellent or very good.
As in:

'My tracky pants look blazin' when I tuck them into my socks.'

See also *bad, bo, gnarly, gravy, heavy, mint, nang, off the hook,
phat, rude, safe, shibby, shiznit, sick, tidy, tight.*

bling

Term coined by *gangsta* rappers that attempts to imitate the
'sound' of light reflecting from jewellery, which came to be
associated with the jewellery itself and the wealthy lifestyle of
someone who wears it. Contrary to popular belief, however,
you cannot be bling just by wearing any type of jewellery.

See also Mingin' or Blingin', page 87.

blinglish

Modern, spoken English. A complex and rapidly changing
language that you will be ridiculed for failing to understand.

blood clart

West Indian patois insult, not meaning 'blood clot', as is
sometimes assumed, but 'blood cloth', i.e. a sanitary towel.

bloods

LA gang who wear red and are the arch enemies of the *crips*.

blows

US term to describe something as rubbish or crap;
confusingly, if something blows, it probably *sucks* too. As in:

'Double Geography blows.'

See also *budget, lame, sucks, unsafe, wack, weary.*

blud

A friend. As in:

'You alright for pills tonight, blud?'

See also *bredrin, brother, clart, dogg, moosh, spa.*

blunt

A cigar hollowed out and filled with marijuana to disguise the drug-taking from passing police. Because everyone knows that teenagers like nothing better than a cigar to go with their evening bottle of Strongbow.

bo

Something good or cool, popularized by the TV show *Bo' Selecta!*, as were 'boo shank' and 'shat pang'. As in:

'My new ringtone is well bo.'

See also *bad, blazin', gnarly, gravy, heavy, mint, nang, off the hook, phat, rude, safe, shibby, shiznit, sick, tidy, tight.*

bomb

- Something that is cool or the best. As in:

'This White Lightning is *da* bomb.'

- To curl into a ball while jumping into a swimming pool, so you cause as big a splash as possible. Which is also pretty cool.

boo

A boyfriend or girlfriend. Someone you have serious feelings about, rather than just a *fuckbuddy*.

See also *wifey*.

SOUND CONFUSION WARNING

booming

The hip-hop equivalent of cheering. It involves chanting the word 'boom', and sounds confusingly similar to booing. So if you are a badass *gangsta* rapper, or are considering becoming one, don't get too upset if it sounds like the crowd are booing you.

booty

A girl's arse.

booty call

Not a phone call made to a girl's arse, but a phone call made with the intention of seducing someone.

bootylicious

Voluptuous, curvaceous, or attractive. The line between bootylicious and fatass is a fine one, and pretty much down to individual taste.

booyakasha

A gangsta exclamation that's now only used by people doing impressions of Ali G. According to a popular urban myth, it secretly means 'death to all white people', but it's actually supposed to suggest the sound of gunshot.

borrow

Blinglish for 'lend'. As in:

'Can you borrow me a fiver until giro day?'

See also *lend*.

bo selecta

Literally translates as 'Good DJ', but it's unlikely that anyone would use this earnestly since the TV show featuring Avid Merrion.

bothered

Word said sarcastically to show you don't care about something. Alternatives include, 'Am I bothered though?', 'Do I look bothered?' and 'Does this face look bothered to you?' As in:

Teenager 1: Trevor P just said you was a slag.

Teenager 2: Bothered.

bounce

- To leave. As in:

'Here comes the truancy officer. Let's bounce.'

- To drive. From *gangstas* bouncing their low riders up and down on hydraulic motors, which might look pretty cool but makes it harder for the person in the passenger seat to navigate or serve tea from a Thermos flask.

boys

Friends. As in:

'I *licked* Dwayne B in his face on Thursday. But it's alright, we're boys again now.'

bra

Welsh or West country variation of 'bro', 'bruv' or 'brother'.
A friendly greeting, rather than a comparison to an over-the-
shoulder-boulder-holder. As in:

'You're fucking *safe*, bra.'

brap! brap!

An all-purpose exclamation of excitement. Can denote
anything from hearing a favourite garage anthem to seeing
someone slip over.

breaded

To be rich. As in:

'Brendan has a Nintendo DS and a PSP. He must be properly
breaded.'

See also *minted*.

bredrin

A friend – 'brethren' pronounced with a stereotypical West
Indian accent.

See also *blud, brother, clart, dogg, moosh, spa.*

breezer gut

Female beer gut. As displayed by *chavettes* who see their weight issues as no barrier to wearing short tops, and originates from the popular *chavette* drink, Bacardi Breezer.

brick shithouse

Stocky and well-built. A Northern term comparing someone to an outdoor toilet. A compliment to a man, an insult to a woman.

brother

A friendly term used mainly by black males, although some *wiggas* might use it too. Can be shortened to 'bro' or 'bruv' when greeting someone. 'Cuz', as in 'cousin', is also used similarly.

See also *blud, bredrin, clart, dogg, moosh, spa.*

budget

Something cheap and poor quality, like trainers from the market. Also used more generally, to refer to anything rubbish.

See also *blows, lame, sucks, unsafe, wack, weary*.

buff

Attractive, *fit*. As in:

'Justin Timberlake is buff, you know.'

See also *fit*.

bum

- Arse.
- To do someone up the arse.
- A tramp.
- To beg like a tramp.

bumfuck

A US term to describe somewhere in the middle of nowhere.
Also known as the 'asscrack of nowhere'. As in:

'She's a little slow. She's from Bumfuck, Nebraska.'

bum ting

Someone attractive or good-looking. As in:

'Bum ting at three o'clock.'

bunny boiler

A possessive woman. From the scene in *Fatal Attraction*
where Glenn Close boils the pet rabbit. As in:

Bloke 1: That's the third text she's sent me since I got off with her.

Bloke 2: Uh-oh. Sounds like a bunny boiler to me.

burberry

One of those clothing brands like Hackett that's only worn by
very posh and very *pikey* people.

burbarian

A violent person who wears *Burberry*, a *chav*.

See also Modern Portmanteau Words, page 54.

bust a cap

To shoot someone. As in:

'If I see someone from the North Gerard's Cross *posse* on our turf, I'll bust a cap in they ass.'

butters

Ugly, *minging*. Hip-hop slang. As in:

'How can they call themselves the Sugababes when they're all so butters?'

buzzin'

Something that's excellent or someone who's high. As in:

'Me and Ricky J spent the whole of General Studies sniffing Tippex and now we're buzzin'.'

Minger Spotting 1 – Birds

If you can tick all the characteristics below then congratulations –
you've spotted a genuine *Wife Swap*-class Ming the Merciless.

A *pram face* ◯

A short top exposing a *breezer gut* ◯

A fake designer handbag ◯

A *Croydon facelift* ◯

A *visible thong strap* ◯

Minger Spotting 2 – Blokes

A male version of the minger-spotting guide,
in the interests of fairness.

Baseball cap ◯

Hoodie ◯

Fake designer clothing ◯

Nuff market *bling* ◯

Bumfluff tache ◯

C

cane

- To drink or take drugs.

- To do something quickly. As in:

'I was late for meeting her, so I had to cane some *maccy ds*.'

caner

Someone who takes lots of drugs or drinks lots of alcohol.

See also *waster*.

cashback!

Exclamation of victory popularized by Alan Partridge. As in:

'I've just been promoted to assistant team leader. Cashback!'

See also *back of the net!*, *get in!*, *kiss my face!*.

cash money

Money in the form of notes rather than credit cards, debit cards or cheques. The coolest form of money to have, seeing as though you can't use Switch with pimps, dealers and that Chinese bloke down the pub who sells cigs and pirate DVDs.

cha

West Indian-derived expression of disgust, an alternative to the act of teeth-kissing. As in:

'What you being such a chief for? Cha, man.'

See also *kissing your teeth*.

charver

A chav from the north-east of Britain. Also known as a 'radgie' or a 'twocker'; the latter originates from the acronym 'Taken Without Owner's Consent'.

See also *chav, kev, ned, scally, schemie, spide, townie*.

chav

A sportswear-clad member of the British underclass, also known as a *charver*, *kev*, *ned* or *townie*. The word 'chav' derives from 'chavi', the Romany word for 'child', rather than an acronym like 'Council Housing Association Vermin', as is sometimes claimed.

Chavs were first identified in Chatham in Kent, but have since gone on to become the biggest social phenomenon of recent years. Either a genuine social menace or just an excuse for the middle class to laugh at working-class people, depending on your point of view.

See also *charver*, *kev*, *ned*, *scally*, *schemie*, *spide*, *townie*.

chavette

A female *chav*. Probably clad in the same kind of sportswear as a male *chav*, but might add feminine touches like scrunchies, a fake Louis Vuitton handbag and a bright orange tan.

See also *kappa slappa*.

chaviar

Used to describe any food that *chavs* love, such as Kansas Fried Chicken and meat kebabs.

chavling
A *chav* child. The kind of kid you see drinking alcopops on swings and letting off bangers near old people in the shopping centre.

chip off
To leave. As in:

'I'm gonna chip off now. I've got *manoeuvres* to make.'
See also *bail, bounce, dip out, do one, rock and roll*.

check it
A directive to 'look over there'. Used in situations such as driving past a hottie while cruising in your Nova.

cheddar / cheese
Money. From the historical practice of giving free cheese as well as money to those on benefits in the US. As in:

'I've got a bit of cheddar today. Let's go down the Arndale.'

See also *benjamins, cream, dead presidents, dollars, franklins, notes, papers*.

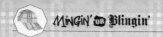

Words That Have Changed Their Meaning Twice

WORD	ONCE MEANT...	THEN MEANT...	NOW MEANS...
buff	to polish something	naked	attractive
chronic	of long duration, or recurring	rubbish	strong weed
gay	bright or lively	homosexual	rubbish
heavy	having great weight	distressing	good
kicks	blows made by feet	thrills or fun	trainers
punk	prostitute	Sex Pistols fan	to play a practical joke on someone
pussy	cat	vagina	coward
sick	unwell	in poor taste	good

chicken

- Someone who won't join in *chavling* dares like dropping paving stones off bridges or standing in the traffic. Not to be used when addressing Marty McFly.

- Affectionate term of address, as used by Geordie *Chavette* Michelle from *Big Brother 5*.

chickenhead

A woman who gives blow jobs. From the motion of a head bobbing up and down like a chicken's head.

WORD CONFUSION WARNING

chief

Please note that if someone calls you 'chief', they might be using a slightly old-fashioned friendly greeting. However, if someone calls you 'a chief', they are calling you a twat.

So if someone greets you with, 'Alright, chief?' you should smile and reply politely. However, if someone greets you with, 'Alright, you chief?' you should reply, 'What are you calling me a chief for? You're the one who's a fucking chief.'

choke

To fail or lose at something. Especially used within the context of losing an argument because you couldn't think of a good comeback fast enough. This sentiment can also be emphasized by coughing and putting your hands around your throat. As in:

> Schoolkid 1: Your mum's so fat the lift says, 'Maximum capacity: 8 persons or your mum.'
>
> Schoolkid 2: Errmmmm . . .
>
> Everyone watching: Aaaahh . . . choked!
>
> See also Modern Sign Language, page 00.

chronic

Once used to describe something that wasn't very good. Now describes any strain of marijuana that *is* very good.

> See also Words That Have Changed Their Meaning Twice, pg 36.

chuggers

A contraction of 'charity muggers', those frighteningly pushy charity collectors who are paid to stand in your way and ignore your claim to be in a bit of a hurry.

clart

A mate. Derived from West Indian insults like *blood clart* and *raas clart*, in which 'clart' actually means 'cloth'. As in:

'It's fucking *tidy*, clart.'

See also *blud*, *bredrin*, *brother*, *dogg*, *moosh*, *spa*.

click

A group, from the word 'clique'. As in:

'I spent last night drinking Strongbow in Aldi car park with my click.'

See also *massive*, *posse*.

clock

To notice, look at or hit something (or someone). As in:

'I clocked him clocking me so I clocked him.'

clocking

The practice of pointing out the location of attractive

members of the opposite sex to your friends by calling out clock-hand positions, like 'three o'clock' and 'nine o'clock'.

cock blocker

A friend who stops you getting off with someone you fancy by being dorky or simply failing to take the hint and go away. The opposite of a *wingman*.

coffin dodger

An elderly person. As in:

> 'Sorry I took so long. I got stuck behind a coffin dodger at the cashpoint.'

coinage

Coins, or a small amount of money. As in:

> 'By the time we got to *maccy ds*, I only had coinage left.'

> See also *shrapnel*.

cotchin'

Hanging around or relaxing. Can be done anywhere from the

40

jacuzzi in an exclusive penthouse suite to the bench in front of the village war memorial. Not to be confused with *cottaging* (see below).

See also *liming*.

cottaging

To seek out gay sex in public toilets. The presence of glory holes drilled in the partition walls of toilet cubicles is a good sign that you're in a cottaging hotspot.

cracker

A white person. Derived from the cracking whips of the slave owners in eighteenth-century America.

See also *honky*, *whitey*.

craptacular

A US term meaning something spectacularly crap, popularized by Bart Simpson. Often used to refer to things that are so bad they're actually good. Variations include 'craptastic' and 'craptabulous'.

cream

- Semen. As in:

  'Alright, calm down, don't cream yourself.'

- Money. From the acronym 'Cash Rules Everything Around Me'.

See also *benjamins, cheddar, dead presidents, dollars, franklins, notes, papers*.

crib

A home. Conjures images of cool waterfront apartments thanks to MTV's TV show *Cribs*, but it's more likely to refer to a bedroom in a suburban semi-detached house. As in:

'Let's go back to my crib and play *GTA San Andreas*.'

crips

- An LA gang who wear blue and are the arch enemies of the *bloods*. The origin of the name is not known, although one theory claims that the name derives from gang members walking with a limp (see *pimp roll*). Some

unlikely acronyms have also been suggested, such as
'Cowards Run In Packs'.

See also Acronym Myths, page 127.

- *Blinglish* for 'crisps'.

cristal

Louis Roederer Cristal champagne. A *bling* drink.

Croydon facelift

Hair that's scraped back so tight it stretches the skin. Often
created using strong hairspray and a scrunchie. The *chavette*
hairstyle of choice.

WORD CONFUSION WARNING

cruise

Can either mean to drive around pointlessly in your mate's
Vauxhall Nova and shout things at girls, or to seek gay sex
in a park. So be sure to check what kind of cruising you've
just agreed to participate in.

crunk

Intoxicated, wild, or excited. An amalgam of the phrase 'crazy drunk'. Also refers to a genre of hip-hop music.

See also Modern Music Genres, page 138.

D

da

Blinglish for 'the'.

dan

Blinglish for 'than'.

dapper

Well dressed. A word that's only used by very old and very young people. Although in its modern use it probably refers to box-fresh white trainers and a hoodie pulled up over a baseball cap rather than a Savile Row suit and a bowler hat.

dash

To throw something violently. As in:

'Jason just dashed his *KFC* box all over a car windscreen.
It was *jokes*.'

Modern Rhyming Terms	
EXPRESSION	**MEANING**
beaver leaver / vagina decliner / bum chum	a homosexual
cock block	someone or something that prevents you from copping off
fag hag	a straight woman with close gay male friends
hag fag	a gay man with close female friends
kappa slappa	a *chavette*
spac attack	a fit of violent rage
todger dodger	a lesbian
tyre fryer	a boy racer
yummy mummy	an attractive older woman, a *milf*

dat

Blinglish for 'that'.

dead

A word used primarily by Northerners to mean 'very'. As in:

'You're dead nice, you.'

See also *proper*, *pure*, *well*.

dead presidents

Money. From the presidents who appear on US banknotes. 'Dead composers, scientists and philanthropists' would be more accurate in the UK (though less catchy).

See also *benjamins*, *cheddar*, *cream*, *dollars*, *franklins*, *notes*, *papers*.

denied

The word used to tease someone who's just been blown out by a member of the opposite sex.

Bloke: Well, she said she already had a boyfriend.

Mates: Deeeniiiiied!

See also *air*, *blank*.

dip out

To leave.

See also *bail, bounce, chip off, do one, rock and roll.*

dis

Blinglish for 'this'.

diss

To insult somone, and derived from 'disrespect'. Covers everything from a cutting rhyme delivered by one rapper who has *beef* with another, to telling someone during maths that their mum has a cock.

disco vicar

An uncool (or old) person trying to be cool.

diva

A difficult woman, or gay man, who must have everything exactly their way. From the alleged behaviour of stars such as J-Lo and Mariah Carey.

dog / dogg

When spelt with one 'g' it refers to a *minger*. When spelt
with two 'g's it becomes hip-hop speak for 'friend'. So make
sure a girl is hip-hop literate before greeting her with,
'Wassup, dogg?'

dogging

The act of having sex in a public place, often with
strangers looking on. The term derives from the excuse of
those observing that they were just walking their dog when
they happened to see the act taking place. Which is about
as convincing as the excuse that they were hoovering in
the nude when they slipped and fell on the nozzle.

dollars

A UK term for money, using the US word. As in:

'I wanted that new McKensie hoodie from JD on Saturday, but
I didn't have enough dollars.'

See also *benjamins, cheddar, cream, dead presidents, franklins, notes, papers.*

dom p
Dom Perignon champagne. Another *bling* drink.

don
Someone who is respected or admired. Derived from the term for a mafia boss.

do one
To leave. As in:

'Why don't you just fucking do one?'

See also *bail, bounce, chip off, dip out, rock and roll.*

dope
Marijuana, heroin, or simply anything cool or great. As in:

'Woah, this dope is, like, dope.'

do what?

Means, 'Pardon?' Used to express disbelief in Estuary English. As in:

Newsagent: That will be £2.75 please.

Geezer: Do what?

down

An expression of understanding or agreement. As in:

Playa 1: Why don't we go to the precinct and hang out in Tennessee Fried Chicken?

Playa 2: Yeah, I'm down with that.

do you want a medal? / do you want a chufty badge?

Rhetorical questions addressed to someone who's boasting about something especially unimpressive.

See also *aren't you just the man*?

drug-fucked

To be high, trashed, fried, baked, cranked, monged, or *mashed up* on drugs, or ruined the day(s) after.

duh

An appropriate response to someone who's just stated the obvious; a more modern and American-sounding alternative to the classic, 'No shit, Sherlock.' As in:

Teenager 1: Apparently Julian is gay.

Teenager 2: Like . . . duh.

dutty

The word 'dirty' spoken in a West Indian accent. Now used as a compliment, rather than as a reference to someone's body odour or inappropriate language.

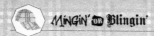

E

easy now

- An alternate way of saying 'calm down'.
- A greeting. As in:

'Easy now, Dave.'

ends

Your local area. As in:

Bad boy: What ends you *repping*?

Wannabe bad boy: Royal Tunbridge Wells.

See also *manor*, *round our way*, *village*.

evils

Dirty (i.e. aggressive) looks. As in:

'She started it. She was giving me evils.'

extra

Unnecessary or over-the-top behaviour. As in:

'What are you being so extra for?'

F

fabulous

Anything that gay men like. As in:

'I really respect Cher for what she's been through. She's fabulous.'

facety

Being cheeky or rude (that's impolite, not *rude*). As in:

Kappa slappa 1: Your mum walks like John Wayne.

Kappa slappa 2: Don't get facety with me.

fag hag

A woman with close gay male friends. Can often be found in trendy bars, despairing about being unable to find a bloke who's as sensitive, attractive and fashion-conscious as her fabulous *GBF*.

See also *GBF*, *hag fag*, *lesbro*.

Modern Portmanteau Words

bling + English = **Blinglish**

burberry + barbarian = **burbarian**

chav + caviar = **chaviar**

charity + mugger = **chugger**

crap + fantastic = **craptastic**

crazy + drunk = **crunk**

dire + dialogue = **direlogue**

faux + bohemian = **fauxhemian**

fucking + ugly = **fugly**

grab + yank = **gank**

iPod + spod = **iSpod**

mock + cockney = **mockney**

shit + glitterati = **shitterati**

straight + *gay* = **stray**

squeegee + mugger = **squgger**

twat + cunt = **twunt**

wack + *gangsta* = **wanksta**

WORD CONFUSION WARNING

fat one

Can refer to a large marijuana spliff or a large penis, so be sure to check what exactly it is you've just agreed to suck on.

fat whacker

Northern term for a fat person, or *salad dodger*.
Variations include 'fat knacker', 'fat waster' and the
Pop Idol-inspired 'fat Waller'.

feelin'

Enjoying or appreciating something. As in:

'I'm feeling these new windscreen-washer lights you've put in.'

fill yer boots

Northern expression meaning 'go ahead', or 'help yourself'.
As in:

Northerner 1: Can I have some of your chips and gravy?
Northerner 2: Fill yer boots.

fit

Attractive. Can also include being in good physical
shape in the more traditional sense of the word.

See also *buff*.

flakey

Unreliable or absent-minded. As in:

'Sorry, I'm being a bit flakey today. I'm still *drug-fucked* from last night.'

flexing

- US hip-hop speak for gloating, showing off or bigging yourself up.

- UK chav speak for annoying someone. As in:
'Stop flexing me. *Footballers' Wives* is on.'

for real

- A *townie* expression for agreeing with someone.

- An alternative to *safe*, *believe* or 'I'm *down* with that'.

fo' shizzle my nizzle

The most famous example of 'izzle speak', literally 'for sure my nigga', a term of agreement meaning 'yes', or 'that's fine'.

See also Izzle Speak, page 70.

franklins

Money. An obvious variation on *benjamins*.

See also benjamins, cheddar, cream, dead presidents, dollars, notes, papers.

freak

- A word *townies* use when insulting *moshers* and *grebs*. As in:

  'Oi freak! Shut your mouth or I'll shut it for you!'

- To have sex. But not necessarily with a *mosher* or a *greb*.

frontin'

Pretending to be something you're not to impress others. For example, someone who aspires to the *gangsta* lifestyle, but hasn't even bothered to shoot anyone yet is 'frontin''.

frosted

Someone dripping with jewellery, or displaying *nuff bling*.

fubar

US word meaning 'drunk', also, an acronym of 'Fucked Up Beyond All Recognition', either from drink or drugs.

fuck / fuckin'

A swear word with a wide range of meanings and usage, but now increasingly used as a replacement for 'err' or 'umm' while trying to think of a word. As in:

'She said she'd meet us in fuckin' … whatdoyoucallit … fuckin' … yates's at nine.'

fuckbuddy

A friend with whom you've agreed to have a purely sexual relationship, without the danger of emotional attachment or exclusivity.

fuck off

Many uses, including:

- 'Go away', or 'get lost'.
- 'Don't push your luck.'

- 'I don't believe you.'
- Large.

  See also *big-massive-no-way-fuck-off*.

- An alternative to 'hang on', 'hang about', or 'what did you say?' in the North. As in:

  'Fuck off a minute, she said what?'

fugly

A contraction of the words 'fucking' and 'ugly'. The most mingingest *minger* in town.

See also *biffa, gipper, gonk, minger, munter, swamp donkey, ug, wouldn't touch her with yours*.

G

game

Someone's skills or abilities. As in:

'Gordon's got no game.'

gangsta

A *bad boy* from the *ghetto* who *keeps it real*. As opposed to a *wanksta*, or someone who's just pretending to live this lifestyle. Sometimes shortened to 'G'.

gangsta limp

The fake limp that people adopt to look hard, also known as the *pimp roll*. Can be supplemented by grabbing your crotch or making a *gangsta* hand gesture.

See also Modern Sign Language, page 78.

gank

To steal. Covers everything from hotwiring a car to merely pretending to put money into the honesty boxes in WH Smith when grabbing a copy of the *Sun* in the morning.

See also *jack, tax, teef, thug*.

gash

Women.

WORD CONFUSION WARNING

gay

As if it wasn't confusing enough for old people that the word they want to use to describe a beautiful spring morning also means homosexual, the word 'gay' is now used to refer to anything pathetic or stupid. As in:

'Nigel's new jacket is so gay.'

See also Words That Have Changed Their Meaning Twice, page 36.

gaydar

An intuitive ability to tell if someone is homosexual. Could be based on an unknown and supernatural sixth sense, or just on the fact that the bloke in question is wearing a tight vest top and singing 'I Will Survive' at karaoke.

gaymo

A word combining 'gay' and 'homo' to imply double gayness. As in:

'Tony's such a gaymo. If he was a wizard, he'd be Gandalf the Gay.'

GBF

An acronym of 'Gay Best Friend'. An essential accessory for any modern *fag hag*. Not to be confused with the BFG, who was almost certainly heterosexual.

See also *fag hag, hag fag, lesbro*.

get horizontal

To have sex. Alternatives include 'horizontal boogie', 'horizontal hula' and 'horizontal mambo'.

See also *freak, get jiggy, ride*.

get in!

An exclamation of victory, used mainly in the South. Now often substituted by an Alan Partridge-inspired variation such as *back of the net!*, *cashback!* or *kiss my face!*.

get jiggy

To have sex. As in:

'How's about getting jiggy with Mr Biggy?'

See also *freak, get horizontal, ride*.

ghetto

An impoverished inner-city area. And by association, anything that is cool, urban or *gangsta*.

See also *hood*, *projects*.

ghetto fabulous

Something that's particularly cool in an urban or *gangsta* way. Sounds like it should refer to a gay *gangsta* rapper, but there doesn't seem to be much need for a term to describe this. I mean, it's supposed to be about 1 in 10, isn't it? Surely one of them must be.

gift of fire

A *wanky* way of asking someone if they have a light. As in:

'Have you got the gift of fire, mate?'

gipper

An ugly woman, a *minger*. As in:

'I can't make up my mind about whether that Sarah Jessica Parker is a gipper or not.'

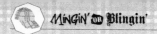

See also *biffa, fugly, gonk, minger, munter, swamp donkey, ug, wouldn't touch her with yours*.

glove

A condom. As in:

'No love without the glove. Let's stop off at the all-night garage.'

gnarly

Means 'great' or 'cool', and derived from US skater speak. As in:

'Let me push you down the steps in this shopping trolley. It'll be gnarly.'

See also *bad, blazin', bo, gravy, heavy, mint, nang, off the hook, phat, rude, safe, shibby, shiznit, sick, tidy, tight*.

goes

Blinglish for 'said'. As in:

'So I goes to him, "I don't care who she is, you're chucked".'

gonk

An idiotic and *minging* person. An insult that compares someone to a cheap fairground prize made out of fur and toilet-roll tubes.

grab a granny

A bar or club that attracts older clientele, such as 'Divorcees' Night' at your local *meatmarket*. As in:

'It's grab-a-granny night at Destiny's tonight, so it should be *well* easy to pull.'

gravy

- Something good, *safe* or *mint*. As in:

  'That Fila top looks *well* gravy.'

- An expression of contentment or satisfaction. As in:

  'It's all gravy.'

  See also *bad, blazin', bo, gnarly, heavy, mint, nang, off the hook, phat, rude, safe, shibby, shiznit, sick, tidy, tight.*

greb

Someone who's into goth, emo or alternative music and wears black. Regarded as *freaks* by *chavs*. Derived from 'greebo', which was a popular slang term in the nineties.

See also Modern Music Genres, page 138.

gullible

This word has been removed from the dictionary.

gwan

Exclamation of excitement derived from 'go on'. As in:

'Gwan with your *bad* self.'

gyppo (or gippo)

A financially poor or unclean person. Sometimes shortened to 'gyp'. As in:

'Your mum's so gyp that she hangs the toilet paper out to dry.'

See also *pikey*, *scav*.

H

hag fag

A gay man with many close female friends.

See also *fag hag*, *GBF*, *lesbro*.

happy slapping

Using a camera phone to record yourself or your mates *handing out some slaps* to random members of the public. Not a good thing.

hand out some slaps

To hit someone. As in:

'Any time that chief comes near me I'm gonna hand out some slaps, you know.'

See also *beats*, *licks*, *open a can of whoopass*, *smack down*, *spark*, *tumps*.

hang a left / right

An instruction to turn left or right. Often overhead when a

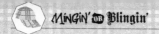

trendy in your vicinity is giving someone directions over the phone.

hanging

A word meaning 'ugly' or 'disgusting', and predominantly used in the North and in Wales. As in:

'I wouldn't even snog him for a million pound – he's hanging.'

happy shopper

A downmarket, cheap version of something else, and even worse than being the *tesco value* version of something. As in:

'Vinnie Jones is the happy shopper Vin Diesel.'

See also tesco value.

hardcore

Anything intense or extreme. Can also refer to US rock and British techno music, or Swedish movies.

heavy

Former hippy-speak to describe a serious or distressing situation. Now it just means something good. As in:

'That bit where he beat up those twenty guys at once was heavy, you know.'

See also *bad*, *blazin'*, *bo*, *gnarly*, *gravy*, *mint*, *nang*, *off the hook*, *phat*, *rude*, *safe*, *shibby*, *shiznit*, *sick*, *tidy*, *tight*.

heffa

A hefty woman, such as Ann Widdecombe, Michelle McManus or Fern Britton.

hella

A contraction of 'a hell of a lot of', or simply meaning 'very'. As in:

'Tyrique's wearing his jeans hella low today. You can see his fake Calvin Kleins.'

See also *bare*.

hen

Hennessey cognac. Good to bring to a party if you want to look *bling*.

Izzle Speak

Slang-speak popularized by US rapper Snoop Dogg which involves substituting 'izzle' for the ends of words.

For example:
'For sure my nigga' becomes 'fo' shizzle my nizzle'.

'Off the hizzle' – 'off the hook'.
'Smoke a jizzle' – 'smoke a joint'.

Warning: It's quite difficult to stop doing this once you've started. A popular variation on this uses 'eezy' as the word ending instead, for example, 'fo' sheezy my neezy', and 'off the heezy'. This kind of slang is very handy for rappers, as it can make any words rhyme. However, it's worth remembering that it doesn't work for words that already end that way. As in:

Gangsta 1: What's the weather like today, dogg?
Gangsta 2: Drizzle my nizzle, breezy my neezy.

here (or 'ere)

Chav speak for 'excuse me'. As in:

"Ere mate! Got a fag?'

high-rising terminals

The rising intonation at the end of a sentence, so that every statement sounds like a question? The speech affectation of a generation who have grown up watching US and Australian TV shows?

ho

Whore, prostitute, or any *skanky* woman. Can also be used to refer to women in general, but this is probably unwise in your Feminism Studies tutorial group.

See also *skank*.

holla

To speak, but doesn't necessarily mean to shout. As in:

'Holla at me later.'

WORD CONFUSION WARNING

homie

Please note that the correct way to refer to a friend or acquaintance in your *hood* is homie or homeboy, *not* homo. So, when greeting a gang of youths hanging around in a rough council estate at night, remember the following:

'Hey homeez, how's it hanging?' – right.

'Hey homos, how's it hanging?' – wrong.

homme

A homosexual man in England. Or any man in France.

honky

A white person. As in:

'I may be a honky, but I'm hung like a donkey.'

See also *cracker*, *whitey*.

hoochie

A promiscuous woman, or a *ho*.

See also *skank*, *sket*.

hoochie mama

A woman who's even more promiscuous than a *hoochie*; a female *mack daddy*.

hood

- The local neighbourhood, and therefore, *ghetto*.

- Thing attached to your sweatshirt that you can pull up over your baseball cap which makes it harder for you to be identified on CCTV cameras.

See also *ghetto*, *projects*.

hoodrat

A *nasty* person or *scuzzbucket* from your local area.

hot

Can refer to an attractive member of the opposite sex, as well as stolen goods. As in:

'My cousin can get iPods for £50, but they're hot.'

hotted up

To beat someone up. As in:

'Shane hotted up this guy who was staring at him in Kebabylon last night.'

how do you like them apples?

Another way of asking the rhetorical question, 'How do you like that?' For example, when kicking someone's arse at *Tekken 5*.

hustler

A person who is good at making money. As in:

'I'm a hustler, baby. I just bought a multipack of Club biscuits for 69p from Asda and then sold them on for 30p each.'

I

I don't got . . .

A US-sounding way of saying 'I haven't got . . .'.

inabit

Blinglish for 'goodbye', which has replaced 'laters', as used by early nineties *Top of the Pops* presenter Tony Dortie.

innit

A contraction of 'isn't it?' Also occasionally used (with no meaning whatsoever) to round off the end of a sentence.

See also *and that*, *ting*.

intit

Northern variation of *innit*. As in:

'It's giro day today, intit?'

ish

A modifier to express 'sort of'. Tacked on to the end of a sentence when you can't make your mind up about something.

it's all good

A reply used to state that everything is fine. Often used to avoid the issue in hand.

Woman: I gave you forty pounds for the leccie bill last month, so how come I've just got sent this final demand?

Bloke: Hey, don't worry. It's all good.

J

jack

To steal. As in:

'I just jacked this PS2 game by ripping the tag off and putting it in my bag.'

See also *gank*, *tax*, *teef*, *thug*.

jigga

An alternative form of the word 'gigolo'. Also, like 'trigga', a popular word with *gangsta* rappers because it rhymes with *nigga*.

joint

- A rolled marijuana cigarette.

- A house or home.

- A bar or nightclub.

- A new rap track.

As in:

'This joint's dead – come back to my joint. We can roll a joint and listen to the new Snoop joint.'

jokes

Something funny. As in:

'Me and Brian fed baking soda to some pigeons on Saturday and made them explode. It was jokes.'

juiced

A word that means 'drunk' in US *Blinglish*, or 'to have sex with' in the UK.

See Words With Different Meanings In the US and the UK, page 11.

Modern Sign Language

▲ Making an 'L' shape with your thumb and index finger and slapping it against your forehead
You're a loser

▲ Making a 'W' shape with your thumbs and index fingers
Whatever

➤ Holding your palm out
Talk to the hand, because the face ain't listening.

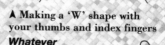

▲ Making an 'M' shape with your thumbs and index fingers
You're a minger

◄ Miming masturbation
You're a wanker.

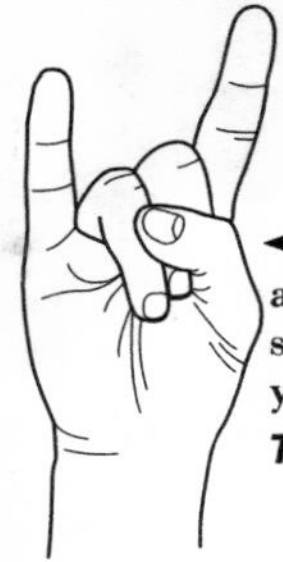

➤ Wiggling your little finger

You've got a small dick

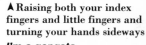

◄ Raising your index finger and little finger to make satanic horns and holding your hand in the air

These guys rock.

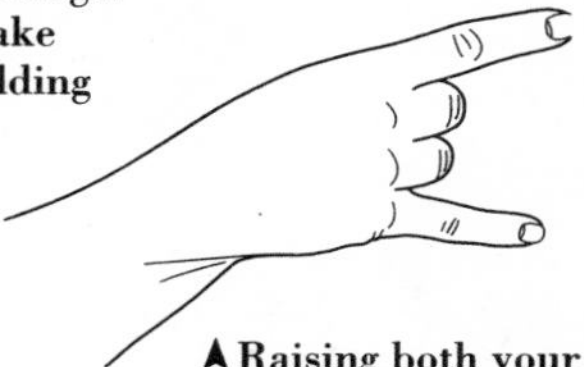

▲ Raising both your index fingers and little fingers and turning your hands sideways

I'm a gangsta

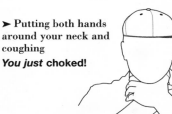

▲ Miming masturbation on your head

You're a dickhead

➤ Putting both hands around your neck and coughing

***You just* choked!**

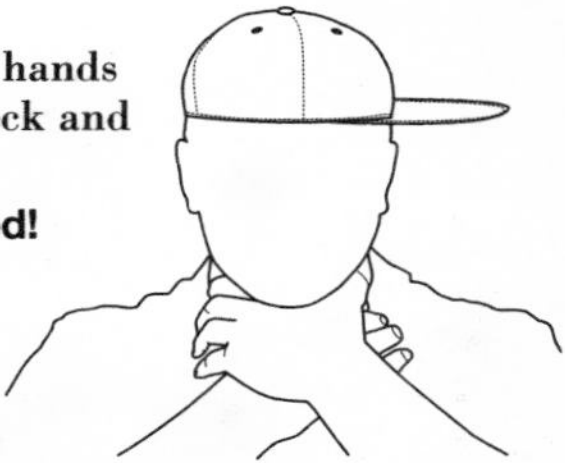

K

kappa slappa

A *pikey* girl who wears Kappa tracksuits.

See also *chavette*.

keep it real

To recommend to someone that they don't pretend to be
what they're not. Sometimes said without a hint of irony by
pretend *gangstas*.

kev

A *chav* from the south-east of England, deriving from the
popular Thames Estuary name of 'Kevin'.

See also *charver, chav, ned, scally, schemie, spide, townie.*

kevved up

- **Someone who's dressed like a *kev*. As in:**

'Darren was kevved up to the max last night – he had on his blue
Adidas tracksuit with fluorescent green stripes.'

- A vehicle that's been *pimped* up *chav*-style, with a spoiler, alloy wheels and a *big-massive-no-way-fuck-off* stereo.

KFC

The Kentucky Fried Chicken fast-food restaurant – the pikiest place on the high street to hang out in if it wasn't for the existence of Kansas Fried Chicken, Tennessee Fried Chicken, LA Fried Chicken and all the other imitation takeaways that cost less, stay open later and attract the kind of clientele who would be refused entry to the local *Poundland* for being too *gyp*.

See also *shit-in-a-tray merchant*.

kicks

Trainers. As in:

Playa 1: How much were those kicks?

Playa 2: They're supposed to be seventy, but my cousin got me them for just twenty quid.

kissing your teeth

The practice of sucking your teeth with your tongue to show either impatience or annoyance with someone.

kiss my face!

Exclamation of victory, popularized by Alan Partridge.

See also *back of the net!*, *cashback!*, *get in!*.

know-what-I-mean?

Rhetorical question now added to the end of most sentences, and generally pronounced as if it were all one word.

L

lairy

To be loud, violent, or rowdy, usually after drinking alcohol. As in:

'Yates's got *well* lairy after you left – these two fat fucks started kicking off.'

lame

A US-sounding word to describe anything stupid, pathetic or rubbish. Used by fourteen-year-old boys about everything except Green Day, Playstations and Angelina Jolie.

See also blows, budget, sucks, unsafe, wack, weary.

largin' it

To have a good time, and a variation of 'havin' it large', which means much the same. As in:

'We were largin' it last night. I had eight lager tops before I moved on to shots.'

lashed

To be exceedingly drunk.

See also leathered, mullered, munted, ratarsed, ripped, wasted.

learn

Curiously, this means to teach someone something. As in:

'I'm gonna have to learn that *chief* not to speak to me like that.'

leathered

Two definitions, both revolving around related topics; the first, to get particularly drunk, and secondly, to be beaten up (heard more in the North of England). As in:

'Darren got leathered on Friday and ended up leathering this student.'

See also *lashed, mullered, munted, ratarsed, ripped, wasted.*

lend

Blinglish for 'borrow'. As in:

'You've lent twenty pound off me this week already.'

See also *borrow.*

lesbro

The male equivalent of a fag hag – a heterosexual man with close lesbian friends.

See also *GBF, fag hag, hag fag.*

licks

Punches. As in:

'If you walked round my way dressed like that, you'd get licks.'

See also *beats, hand out some slaps, open a can of whoopass, smack down, spark, tumps.*

like

One of a few words that can be placed anywhere in a *Blinglish* sentence. Useful for buying time when you're thinking of a witty comeback to an insult:

Kappa slappa 1: You're such a twat.

Kappa slappa 2: Yeah, well, at least . . . like . . . I'm not . . . like . . . a *bitch* like what you are.

liming

A West Indian-derived term that means hanging out or relaxing. As in:

'We spent last night liming outside *Poundstretcher*.'

See also *cotchin'*.

local

Used to describe the *lameness* of small towns, especially
by sixth formers who can't wait to move away to university.
As in:

'You won't see me in *yates's*. It's *well* local.'

See also *village*.

long ting

Describes something that is boring or that takes more time up
than expected. As in:

'That assembly about Gandhi was long ting.'

lord it up

To show off your wealth, or to spend money freely. As in:

'Shane got £700 for his nan dying, so he's lording it up.'

loser

Classic US-derived insult attributing hopeless or pathetic
qualities to an individual. Now used with a corresponding

hand gesture that involves making an 'L' shape with your thumb and index finger.

See also Modern Sign Language, page 78.

Mingin' or Blingin'?	
MINGIN'	**BLINGIN'**
Tiffany & Co. diamond ring	Elizabeth Duke sovereign ring
Bulgari bracelet	Ankle bracelet from the market
Cartier diamond necklace	A pendant in the shape of a teddy bear
Jacob & Co. diamond-encrusted watch	A ganja-leaf medallion with 'chill out' engraved on it
100-carat D-colour flawless diamond	A pair of earrings in the shape of the Nike swoosh
Set of customized gold *spinners* for your Mercedes Benz	A replica of 'the One Ring' from *The Lord of the Rings*, bought from an ad in a Sunday supplement in monthly instalments of £5.99

lush

To describe something of luxury; or, an attractive person.
As in:

'That Paris Hilton is *well* lush. Have you seen the video?'

M

ma

- Hip-hop speak for an attractive woman.

- Someone's mum.

In cases where both meanings apply, the word *milf* should
be used.

mack

A *playa*, or a ladies' man.

mack daddy

Someone who's even more of a *playa* and a ladies' man than a
mack. As in:

'Steve's a right mack daddy. He's got girls hanging off his cock.'

maccy ds

Chav speak for the fast-food restaurant, McDonalds. As in:

'Let's meet in maccy ds at seven before moving on to *yates's* and then Dukes.'

mad

To describe the situation of having or seeing a lot of something. As in:

'There'll be mad *gash* in Elements tonight – it's girls-get-in-free night.'

mad props

To convey your feelings of respect or congratulations to another. As in:

'Mad props to you and your *baby mother* on the birth of your second child.'

manoeuvres

A catch-all term meaning important things you have to do. As in:

'Sorry I'm late. I had manoeuvres to make.'

manor

A Thames Estuary word to describe your local territory. Similar to *turf* in *gangsta*-speak, *ends* in *Blinglish*, and *round our way* in the North.

marga

Skinny. As in:

'She's too marga. It would be like shagging Skeletor.'

mashed up

- **To be high on drugs. As in:**
  'I got mashed up last night. It was great.'

- **To get beaten up. As in:**
  'I got mashed up last night. It was shit.'

massive

A group of people, or gang. As in:

'Big shout going out to the Letchworth Garden City massive.'

See also *click*, *posse*.

maybe where you come from

Northern phrase used to express disbelief at or to rubbish
what someone else is saying. As in:

Girl 1: I think Shane from 4B fancies me.

Girl 2: Yeah, maybe where you come from.

me

Blinglish for 'my'. As in:

'Where's me fucking phone gone? Can you call it, please?'

meatmarket

The *local townie* nightclub, packed full of *chavs* and *chavettes*.
Probably called something like Legends, Monroe's, Elements,
Chasers, Volts, Destiny, Infinity, Dukes or The Zone.

menstrual

An inadvisable word to call a female friend, partner or
relation when they're in a bad mood. As in:

'Alright, so I got off with your best mate. No need to get so menstrual
about it.'

mentalist

An unhinged or unpredictable person. As in:

'You'll get used to Tarquin. He's a complete mentalist.'

milf

An attractive older woman, an acronym for 'Mum I'd Like to Fuck'. Also known as a 'yummy mummy'.

milkshake

The word to describe the qualities a woman possesses that make her attractive to men. The female equivalent of *pimp juice*.

minger

The classic and ubiquitous word to describe a person as ugly. Although anyone who's been brushed with the ugly stick can be described as a minger, there are a few things that mark out a borderline *gipper* from an actual minger. The term also has an associated hand gesture which involves making an 'M' shape with your thumbs and index fingers – see page 78.

See also *biffa, fugly, gipper, gonk, munter, swamp donkey, ug, wouldn't touch her with yours*, Minger Spotting, page 31.

minging (or mingin')
Adjectival form of 'minger' – ugly, or disgusting. Popularized, ironically enough, by Jade Goody from *Big Brother 3*.

mint
Something good or cool. As in:

'My Burberry cap looks mint when I wear it at a 45-degree angle.'

See also *bad, blazin', bo, gnarly, gravy, heavy, nang, off the hook, phat, rude, safe, shibby, shiznit, sick, tidy, tight*.

minted
To be rich. As in:

'I spent all Saturday picking up used travelcards and selling them on for a quid, so I'm minted now.'

See also *breaded*.

moby

The abbreviation for 'mobile phone', used by those people who have a picture of Jordan as their wallpaper and the Crazy Frog ring-tone.

mofo

Abbreviation of 'motherfucker' or 'motherfucking'. As in:

'Ayo dad! Pass me the mofo HP sauce!'

moosh

A *chav* word for 'mate' that's derived from 'mush'. As in:

'Oi, moosh! You lookin' at me or chewing a brick? Cos either way you'll get your jaw broken.'

See also *blud, bredrin, brother, clart, dogg, spa*.

mosher

Someone who likes hard rock, metal or US punk music. Derives from the 'mosh pits' that form in front of the stages at such concerts, where the 'dancing' involves jumping on your mates and stage-diving. Moshers have long hair, wear oversized hoodies and baggy jeans, and get called *freaks* by *townies*.

most bestest

Even better than the best. As in:

'Becky is my most bestest friend.'

See also *bestest*.

mug yourself

To do something stupid or self-destructive, like throwing your kebab at a police car.

mullered

Like *leathered*, this word refers both to being drunk, and being duffed up.

See also *lashed, leathered, munted, ratarsed, ripped, wasted*.

munchies

The name of the particular hunger experienced while stoned. Often the kind of thing *disco vicars* mention as proof that they've taken drugs at some point in their lives.

munted

Once again, to be very drunk.

See also lashed, leathered, mullered, ratarsed, ripped, wasted.

munter

An ugly person. As in:

'Eeurrgh! Spin the bottle again! I'm not going with that munter.'

See also biffa, fugly, gipper, gonk, minger, swamp donkey, ug, wouldn't touch her with yours.

my bad

A way of admitting that something is your mistake and apologizing for it. As in:

Teenager 1: I *told* you Ethan was gay.

Teenager 2: My bad.

N

nang

Something excellent. As in:

'My trainers look nang if I leave the laces undone.'

See also *bad, blazin', bo, gnarly, gravy, heavy, mint, off the hook, phat, rude, safe, shibby, shiznit, sick, tidy, tight.*

nan jam
A pedestrian traffic jam caused by slow-walking *coffin dodgers*.

nasty
Someone or something *minging* or unpleasant. As in:

'Sonia off *EastEnders* is *well nasty*. But, confusingly, I'd still do her.'

See also *hoodrat, scuzzbucket.*

ned
A Scottish *chav*.

See also *charver, chav, kev, scally, schemie, spide, townie.*

nice personality
A truly back-handed compliment, usually describing a *fugly* girl.

nigga

A derogatory term for someone of black origin, now used to mean 'friend' by black Americans. Note to clueless wannabe *gangstas* from the home counties: this does not make it okay for white people to say it. Especially if they pronounce it like it ends 'er'.

no drama

An expression to reassure or placate — 'no problems', or 'everything's fine'. As in:

Kev 1: Do you want to make something of it?

Kev 2: No drama, mate.

no way!

A term of surprise or disbelief. As in:

Kappa slappa 1: You know that top what Colleen McLoughlin had on in *Heat* magazine? I seen it down New Look for a fiver.

Kappa slappa 2: No way!

northern monkey

Derogative regional term used by Southerners to refer to Northerners.

See also *southern jessie*.

notes

Estuary-speak for money and cash. As in:

'Twenty notes for that? Don't take the piss.'

See also *benjamins, cheddar, cream, dead presidents, dollars, franklins, papers*.

no, *you* the man

Heartfelt expression of approval of another, and the appropriate reply to *you the man*.

nuff

Contraction of 'enough' – to have plenty of something. As in:

'Nuff man dead for less *dan dat*.'

O

off the hook

Something cool, exciting or happening. Popular variations include 'off the hizzle' and 'off the chain'. As in:

'That party at Shane's nan's flat on Saturday was off the hook.'

See also *bad, blazin', bo, gnarly, gravy, heavy, mint, nang, phat, rude, safe, shibby, shiznit, sick, tidy, tight,* Izzle Speak, pg 00.

old school

Anything from a previous era that is still respected. Originally used to refer to the early origins of hip-hop music. Now used by teenagers to refer to anything that's more than a couple of weeks old. As in:

'I'm mainly into old-school stuff like Nirvana.'

OMG

Acronym for 'Oh My God!' An example of how the mobile-phone texting language sometimes creeps into conversation, as each letter is spelled out. As in:

'OMG, Kyle *so* just looked at me! He is *buff*!'

on his dick

Used to describe someone who is infatuated with another or is brown-nosing them. As in:

'You're so on his dick. That's the third time you've texted him today.'

on the rebound

- The state you're in just after being dumped by someone.
- The excuse you give for getting off with an absolute *munter* or going to your local *grab-a-granny* night alone.

open a can of whoopass

To beat someone up. As in:

'Give me my WWF magazine back, Kenneth. Don't make me open a can of whoopass on you.'

See also *beats, hand out some slaps, licks, smack down, spark, tumps*.

out!

US-sounding way of ending a conversation. As in:

Bloke 1: So I'll see you in *yates's* at seven, then.

Bloke 2: Out!

P

pagga

A fight. As in:

'Wayne and Dave are having a pagga in Lidl car park tonight – pass it on.'

papers

Money or cash. As in:

'I've been raking papers since I was promoted to Junior Assistant Team Leader Executive.'

See also *benjamins, cheddar, cream, dead presidents, dollars, franklins, notes.*

peppered

Northern word meaning 'skint', or poor.
As in:

'I'm peppered. I might go down to Asda car park and ask people if I can take their trolleys back for them.'

WORD CONFUSION WARNING

phat

Anything good, cool, or brilliant. Be aware, however, that a *gangsta* hand gesture may be required to avoid potential confusion if you're planning to say to your *ho* or *baby mother* something along the lines of, 'You're looking phat today, dear.'

See also *bad, blazin', bo, gnarly, gravy, heavy, mint, nang, off the hook, rude, safe, shibby, shiznit, sick, tidy, tight,* Modern Sign Language, page 78.

pikey

An even lower-grade version of a *chav*. Take away the

pimped-up Vauxhall Nova and bright white trainers, add a three-litre bottle of White Lightning and you're getting there.

See also *gyppo*, *scav*.

pimp

- A cool and stylish *playa*. Not, in modern usage, someone who finds customers for prostitutes.

- To make something cooler. As in:

  Townie 1: What are you going to do with your lottery winnings?

  Townie 2: Pimp my *ride*.

pimp juice

While it sounds like it should mean *spunk*, it actually means the qualities a *playa* possesses that make him attractive to women.

See also *milkshake*.

pimp roll

To walk with a fake limp like a *gangsta*, implying that you've been shot nine times and survived, like 50 Cent.

See also *gangsta limp*.

Modern Social Groups

We all know about *chavs*, but here are a few more types of people you might want to look out for:

iSpod
An early adopter of new technology who won't stop going on about the new gadget they've just bought.

kidult
A middle-aged person who watches Pixar films, buys Playstation games and reads Harry Potter novels in public.

kippers
Adults who are still supported by their parents. An acronym from 'Kids in Parents' Pockets Eroding Retirement Savings'.

metrosexual
A man who's interested in fashion and his appearance, but who is not actually gay.

middle youth
Someone in their thirties or forties who refuses to give up the youth lifestyle. An 'adultescent'.

nimby
Someone who tries to keep unpleasant things out of their local area. From 'Not In My Back Yard'.

tweenager
A pre-teen who has already adopted the lifestyle of older children, such as text messaging, alcopops and wonderbras.

playa

A cool, wealthy or sexually successful bloke. Someone who is envied by *playa haters*.

playa hater

Sometimes shortened to 'hater', this is an individual who is jealous of your wealth or status. As in:

'Everyone from 3B has been playa hating on me since I copped off with Stacie.'

poontang / pooty / punani

Like *gash*, these exotic terms can be used to refer to 'vagina', or women generally. As in:

'There's *nuff* punani down in Watford. We should go there one night.'

posse

A gang or group of friends. Can be attributed to a group name like the 'Adidas posse', or the 'Netto car park posse'.
But shouldn't.

See also *click, massive.*

postal

Going 'postal' refers to any unprovoked act of violence, and originates from the killing sprees embarked on by several US postal workers over the years. However, can be used in more mundane contexts, such as, 'Barry went postal on me when I put his lunch box on the radiator during Maths.'

poundland

A bargain-basement shop frequented by those who can't even afford *Poundstretcher*.

poundstretcher

A *skanky* shop that *gyppos*, *pikeys* and *kappa slappas* shop in.

pram face

Describes the face of a girl who looks like she should be pushing a pram around a council estate.

prang
To be scared. As in:

'I'm not prang of that dickhead. I can do karate.'

projects
Poor, inner-city housing areas, usually in US cities, often where many rap and hip-hop stars grew up. Note to fifteen-year-olds in the home counties: your parents' five-bedroom suburban house is *not* in the projects.

See also *ghetto*, *hood*.

proper
An expression meaning 'very' or 'much', used primarily by Northerners. As in:

'I think you're proper fit. How's about going twos up on a bastard?'

See also *dead*, *pure*, *well*.

props
A contraction of '*proper respect*'. As in:

'You didn't stand a chance with her, but I got to give you props for trying.'

punk-ass bitch

An insult used by fourteen-year-old skate kids in the home counties who feel that they've done something with their day whenever they say something American.

pure

Means 'lots of', or 'very'. As in:

'There was pure *poontang* in Infinity last night.'

See also *dead*, *proper*, *well*.

pussy

The comic potential of a word that means both 'vagina' and 'cat' was exhausted in seventies' comedies such as *Are You Being Served?* Now, it's more likely to be used to refer to a coward or a wimp.

pussy whipped

To be under the thumb of a woman. To be her *bitch*.

Q

quality

Estuary word meaning 'good', 'cool' or 'excellent'. As in:

'That personalized number plate looks facking quality, mate.'

quick ting

West Indian-derived word for something that took less time than expected. The opposite of *long ting*.

R

raas clart

A West Indian insult meaning 'sanitary towel' or 'arse cloth'.

rank

Anything *nasty* or *skanky*. As in:

'You can have the rest of these *tesco value* crisps if you want. They're rank.'

ratarsed
To be drunk.

See also *lashed, leathered, mullered, munted, ripped, wasted.*

raw
Means 'cool' or 'good' in the US, but 'wrong' or 'unacceptable' in the UK.

See also Words With Different Meanings In the US and the UK, page 11.

repping
Blinglish for 'representing', as in acting as a delegate for your *posse* or *hood*, rather than selling cleaning products door-to-door.

respect
Widespread term used to express admiration or support. As in:

Chav 1: Check the new alloys on my XR2.

Chav 2: Respect!

result!

An exclamation of pleasant surprise. As in:

'I just won £2.50 on this scratchcard. Result!'

rewind

Request for a DJ to play a record again, as popularized by the Craig David character in *Bo' Selecta!*

WORD CONFUSION WARNING

ride

This word has several meanings, so beware.

- **A vehicle. As in:**

    'I've just got some *quality* speakers put in my ride.'

- **To have sex. As in:**

    'Come back to my house, baby – I'll ride you like Seabiscuit.'

- **Your current sexual partner. As in:**

    'She's my ride.'

It therefore pays to be especially clear about what you mean when asking someone to *pimp* your ride.

See also *pimp*.

rim

The outer part of a car wheel rather than the unsavoury sexual act. To be properly *bling*, your rims must be fitted with *spinners*.

See also *spinners*.

ripped

To be drunk or high on drugs. As in:

'They had an all-you-can-drink night at *yates's* on Wednesday, so we all got ripped to our tits.'

See also *lashed*, *leathered*, *mullered*, *munted*, *ratarsed*, *wasted*.

road

Anywhere outside. As in:

'If I see him on road, I'm gonna slap him down, and he won't be getting up again neither.'

roasting

A group sexual activity. Primarily popularized by tabloid reports about the activities of footballers, which meant that commentators could no longer say, 'He'll get a real roasting in the dressing room for that.'

rock and roll

A *wanky* way of announcing your departure, derived from the equally *wanky* 'Let's roll'. As in:

'This *joint's* dead anyway. Let's rock and roll.'

See also *bail, bounce, chip off, dip out, do one.*

round our way

A primarily Northern term meaning 'locally'. As in:

'There's fuck all to do round our way.'

See also *ends, manor, village.*

rude

Previously, a word meaning 'ill-mannered', but now means 'attractive and cool'. It's possible to be both, of course, in a treat-'em-mean-keep-'em-keen kind of way.

*See also bad, blazin', bo, gnarly, gravy, heavy, mint, nang, off the
hook, phat, safe, shibby, shiznit, sick, tidy, tight.*

S

sad

Used to describe something as pathetic or geeky. There are
sad hobbies, sad music genres, and, of course, sad people.
These people are not necessarily unhappy; in fact, many of
them have a total lack of self-awareness and are therefore
much happier than the people who call them sad.

safe

- To denote agreement with someone or something.
- Someone meeting *townie* approval.

See also alright.

- Something cool. As in:

'That Nickelson shirt's *well* safe. How much did it set you back?'

See also *bad, blazin', bo, gnarly, gravy, heavy, mint, nang, off the hook, phat, rude, shibby, shiznit, sick, tidy, tight.*

salad dodger

A fat person.

See also *fat whacker.*

savour the flava

A phrase encouraging you to enjoy and appreciate something, often used by MCs. Or by school bullies who've just farted and are holding your head in the affected area.

scally

A *chav* from the north-west of England.

See also *charver, chav, kev, ned, schemie, spide, townie.*

scav

A poor person, derived from the word 'scavenge', referring to such poverty-induced behaviour. Can also mean to scrounge or sponge something. As in:

'Don't think you're gonna scav a crisp off me, cos you're not.'

See also *gyppo*, *pikey*.

schemie

Another word for a Scottish *chav*, derived from 'housing scheme'.

See also *charver*, *chav*, *kev*, *ned*, *scally*, *spide*, *townie*.

scrub

A US term for a *loser* who thinks he's a *playa*. Should not be confused with 'scrubber', a British term for someone who's *well minging*.

scuzzbucket

A dirty, unclean or poor person. Someone who has a shopping trolley and a mattress in their front garden, for example.

See also *hoodrat*, *nasty*.

set

The correct collective noun for keys, knives and twats. As in:

'I hate *moshers*. They're a right set of twats.'

Incidentally, 'set' has the most definitions of any word in the English language, with over 460 listed in the *Oxford English Dictionary*. But 'set of twats' is the only one you really need to know.

sex up

With a rare incursion of politics into street speak, this now means to exaggerate something or make it seem more exciting than it is, in the 'Iraq WMD dossier' sense, rather than to shag or have sex, in the Color Me Badd sense.

sharking

The act of chatting someone up, going on the pull, and of generally pursuing the opposite sex with the determination of a shark pursuing its prey.

See also *trapping*.

shame!

An exclamation used whenever someone else suffers an embarrassment or misfortune. In extreme cases, where a simple 'shame' just isn't enough, it can be lengthened to 'Shameohshameohshameohshame!'

See also Shamefulness Guide, page 119.

Shamefulness Guide

EVENT	SHAME RATING
Falling over in front of a group of lads outside *Poundstretcher*.	Shame!
Running for the bus and having the doors close right in your face.	Shameohshame!
Your parents picking you up from a party at ten o'clock, because that's your bedtime.	Shameohshameohshame!
Accidentally burping into someone's mouth during a game of 'spin the bottle'.	Shameohshameohshameoh shame!
Waking up at a party and realizing that someone's put your hand in a bucket of warm water and gathered everyone around to watch as you pissed your pants.	Shameohshameohshameoh shameohshame!

sheepshagger
Anyone who comes from a more rural area than you do.

shibby
A US word meaning 'cool'. As in:

'Scope out the shibby *spinners* on that SUV.'

shine
A blow job. What *chickenheads* give out. As in:

'Can't complain though. Got a shine in the *KFC* bogs on Friday night.'

WORD CONFUSION WARNING

shit
Please note that this popular word changes its meaning when prefixed by 'the'.

If, for example, someone tells you that you look the shit with your new trainers on, you should thank them.

However, if they just tell you that you look shit with your new trainers on, you should *hand out some slaps*.

shit-in-a-tray merchant

The kind of fast-food takeaway that sells things like the ambiguous 'meat kebab', and that usually specializes in *chaviar*.

See also *KFC*.

shiznit

Anything that is great, or the best. As in:

'These Findus crispy pancakes are the shiznit, mum.'

Incidentally, 'shiznit' was often the word that the BBC used to dub over 'shit' when showing Eddie Murphy films on TV in the eighties.

shorty

An attractive female, of any height. Not to be confused with 'shortarse', which is not a compliment.

shrapnel

Coins, or a small amount of money. As in:

'I wish I hadn't bought her that JD and Coke. I've only got shrapnel left now.'

See also *coinage*.

sick

Now means something that's good or cool, rather than something that Mediawatch UK want to ban. It could be both, of course.

See also *bad, blazin', bo, gnarly, gravy, heavy, mint, nang, off the hook, phat, rude, safe, shibby, shiznit, tidy, tight.*

skank

- A trashy or promiscuous girl. Also known as a 'skank *ho*'.
- To steal. As in:

'Aaron just skanked a Reebok top from JJB.'

skanky

Anything *nasty*, disgusting or *munting*. As in:

'Charlene, guess what Dave did when you left the room? He sniffed your chair, the skanky twat.'

sket

A promiscuous woman. Derived from the West Indian insult 'skettle'.

See also *hoochie, skank*.

skinny

- Knowledge or information about something.

  See also *what the dilly-o?, 411*.

- One of the many words like 'grande' and 'venti' that Starbucks invented so they could charge £3.30 for coffee, something which until recently cost about 70p.

slag juice

Any alcoholic drink for *chavettes*, like Lambrini, Smirnoff Ice and Bacardi *Breezer*. As in:

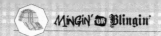 *Mingin' or Blingin'*

'Slag juice is on two-for-one on Wednesdays, so it's *well* easy to cop off.'

smack down
To hit someone. As in:

'Alan, if you don't stop tapping your ruler on the desk, I'm gonna have to put the smack down.'

See also *beats, hand out some slaps, licks, open a can of whoopass, spark, tumps.*

smoke
- **To inhale tobacco, as done by naughty schoolkids.**
- **To shoot someone, as done by really naughty schoolkids.**

smooth
Anything cool. However, often used sarcastically when someone does something clumsy like slipping on an icy pavement or getting their bag caught in a closing bus door.

so
Since *Friends*, a word used by teenaged girls in every

conceivable sentence to emphasize further what is being stated. As in:

'That is *so* not true.'

soldier
A *playa* who has fought their way out of the *ghetto*.

See also *baller*.

solid
Anything good, cool, or brilliant. As in:

'I just bought this solid car stereo for thirty quid down the pub.'

southern jessie
A term used by Northerners to refer to Southerners.

See also *northern monkey*.

spa
A friend. As in:

'Alright spa! You couldn't *borrow* us 50p for the bus home, could you?'

See also *blud, bredrin, brother, clart, dogg, moosh*.

spam

The term given to unsolicited email by geeks, on the grounds that it is as annoying and ubiquitous as the word 'spam' in the famous Monty Python sketch. However, can also be used to refer to any unwanted communication, including talking. As in:

'Stop spamming me. I'm trying to watch Doctor Who.'

spark

A Northern term meaning to punch someone. To 'spark off' is to start a fight; to 'spark out' is to knock someone out with a single blow.

See also beats, hand out some slaps, licks, open a can of whoopass, smack down, tumps.

spide

A *chav* from Northern Ireland.

See also charver, chav, kev, ned, scally, schemie, townie.

Acronym Myths

Although some slang words such as *milf*, *cream* and *fubar* are genuine acronyms, certain words have accrued derivations that are clearly untrue. For example:

Chav = Council Houses And Violence.
Crips = Continuous Revolution In Progress.
Cunt = Can't Understand Normal Thinking.
Fuck = Fornication Under the Command of the King. (Supposedly, the permission to reproduce given by the king.)
Fuck = For Unlawful Carnal Knowledge. (Supposedly, the words written above adulterers held in the stocks.)
Ned = Non-Educated Delinquent.
Pimp = Playa Into Making Progress.
Shit = Super Hot Intestinal Torpedo.

spinners

Additional car rims that continue to spin after your car has stopped moving. An essential addition to your Bentley GT, Hummer or second-hand Fiat Punto.

spunk

As well as referring to man-fat, this word also means
'to waste'. As in:

> 'I lent you fifty quid yesterday. How can you have spunked it already?'

squgger

A contraction of 'squeegee mugger' – the individuals who
wait at traffic lights, cover your windscreen with dirty water
and then ask for money to clean it off. A popular career choice
for *pikeys*.

starting

To initiate a fight. As in:

> Student: Excuse me, could you tell me the way to the student
> union, please?
>
> Local: Are you fucking starting?

. . . 'ster'

A suffix that can be added to the end of any name to create
an instant street nickname, like 'the Davester', 'the Danster'

or 'the Kevster'. In particularly tragic cases, this can be extended further by adding ' . . . meister General', creating 'the Davemeister General'.

straight

Can mean being content with your current situation, or, more commonly, not being homosexual. As in:

> Bloke 1: Do you fancy dressing up as a flamenco girl and miming to a Gloria Gaynor song?
>
> Bloke 2: Nah, I'm straight.

straight up

Used to assert that you're telling the truth, and also a declaration of honest intent. As in:

> 'Did you know, right, that throughout your entire life, your head never actually changes size? Straight up.'

stray

A contraction of 'straight gay', this is a straight man who adopts the mannerisms and lifestyle of a homosexual man. Sometimes a natural expression of someone's inner *fabulousness*, and sometimes just a ruse to cop off with *fag hags*.

stretch

A stretched limousine – a symbol of the *bling* lifestyle, especially if there's a bar, a jacuzzi and a couple of hotties in it. As in:

'Ayo! Put a fresh ice bucket in the stretch.'

stunt

To gloat, or to run your mouth off.

See also *big up*, *flexing*.

sucks

A US term to describe something that's rubbish or pathetic, though, confusingly, it means the same as *blows*.

See also *blows*, *budget*, *lame*, *unsafe*, *wack*, *weary*.

sup?

An abbreviated way of asking someone, 'What's up?' The full-on 'Wassssuuuupppp?' was killed off by the Budweiser advertising campaign some time ago.

swamp donkey

An ugly woman. As in:

> 'How can you say Victoria Beckham's fit? She's a right swamp donkey.'

> See also *biffa, fugly, gipper, gonk, minger, munter, ug, wouldn't touch her with yours*.

sweet

An expression of happiness or contentment. As in:

> 'Oh, wait, the second one's kicking in now. Sweet.'

T

tactical vomiting / tactical chundering

The act of deliberately being sick during all-you-can-drink

nights at your local theme bar. This empties your stomach, allowing more drinking and ensuring that you get your money's worth.

take one for the team

To make a personal sacrifice for the sake of your friends. For example, copping off with a *munter* so your friend can get off with her *fit* mate.

See also *wingman*.

talent

Attractive members of the opposite sex. As in:

'We should go down to Chatham one night. There's pure talent there.'

talk to the hand

This phrase, in conjunction with the gesture of showing someone your palm, means that you've ignored the insulting remark they've just made. As in:

Teenager 1: Is it true that your mum's like a DIY shop – 1p a screw?

Teenager 2: Talk to the hand, because the face ain't listening.

See also Comeback Hierarchy, page 147, Modern Sign Language, page 78.

tax

To steal. As in:

'You can use my pen, but I'm keeping the lid in case you try and tax it.'
See also *gank*, *jack*, *teef*, *thug*.

teef

Again, to steal. From the word 'thief' spoken in a West Indian accent. As in:

'I'm not bringing my PSP into school. There's too many people who'll teef it.'
See also *gank*, *jack*, *tax*, *thug*.

tesco value

A downmarket, cheap imitation of something, originating from Tesco supermarket's 'value' range of food. As in:

'Richard Blackwood is the tesco value Will Smith.'
See also *happy shopper*.

that's what I'm talking about

An expression uttered in satisfaction, when, for example, seeing a hottie walk by, or kicking your mate's arse on *FIFA Street*.

the man

The imaginary enforcer of an establishment whose job it is to preserve the unfair order of things and keep you down. Nobody has ever seen the man, but he probably looks a bit like Peter Bowles in *To the Manor Born*. As in:

> Greb 1: I just removed some of the letters from the STARBUCKS COFFEE sign, so now it says 'FUCK OF'.
>
> Greb 2: Way to stick it to the man!

However, if you are addressed as 'the man', this is a compliment.

See also *you the man*.

thug

To steal. As in:

> 'Jason thugged the alloys off a car outside Netto yesterday.'
> See also *gank, jack, tax, teef*.

tidy

A Welsh term for anything that's cool or great. As in:

'Yates's was fucking tidy last night.'

See also *bad, blazin', bo, gnarly, gravy, heavy, mint, nang, off the hook, phat, rude, safe, shibby, shiznit, sick, tight.*

tight

- **Something cool. As in:**

  'My Von Dutch baseball cap is tight.'

  See also *bad, blazin', bo, gnarly, gravy, heavy, mint, nang, off the hook, phat, rude, safe, shibby, shiznit, sick, tidy.*

- **To be close to others, in a group sense. As in:**

  'Me, Graham and Keith are tight. They my crew.'

ting

Blinglish for 'thing'. Can be used as a more West Indian-sounding version of *and that*. As in:

'I've just been down to Costcutter and ting.'

See also *and that, innit.*

total

A US term meaning to destroy something utterly. As in:

'Corey's grounded for totalling his mom's car.'

touching fists

A gesture rather than an expression – the street equivalent of shaking someone's hand. It involves holding out your fist to someone until they touch it with their fist. Not to be confused with fisting.

townie

A sportswear-clad member of the British underclass.

See also *charver*, *chav*, *kev*, *ned*, *scally*, *schemie*, *spide*.

trapping

Going out on the pull. Northern version of *sharking*.

tumbleweed moment

The moment of embarrassed silence following a bad joke or failed witticism. As in:

136

Bloke 1: How old are you again?

Bloke 2: Thirty-six.

Bloke 1: Well, you don't look a day over forty. (Silence.)

tumps

Hard punches given as punishment to another. Derives from the word 'thump' spoken in a West Indian accent.

See also *beats*, *hand out some slaps*, *licks*, *open a can of whoopass*, *smack down*, *spark*.

tune

A great song. As in:

'Quick! Turn it up! This is a tune!'

turf

Territory marked out by a street gang that is under their 'control'. As in:

'Everything from the front of Aldi to the Mecca Bingo is West Peterborough *massive* turf. If anyone from the East Peterborough *massive* steps on it then . . . blam!'

Modern Music Genres	
Crunk	Rap music from the 'dirty South' of the US, like Lil' John.
Emo	Emotional hardcore. Guitar-driven US rock with a sensitive side, like Jimmy Eat World.
Garage	Underground rock in the US; hip-hop with reggae MCing in the UK.
Grime	A darker and more aggressive offshoot of UK garage, like Wiley or Dizzee Rascal.
Hooligan House	British chav rap pioneered by Mike Skinner, AKA The Streets.
Latte	Radio Two-friendly music like Norah Jones, Katie Melua and Jamie Cullum, made for people who drink milky coffee from Starbucks.

twunt

An insult that suggests two very rude insults without actually being either, which enables it to be used in polite conversation.

See also Modern Portmanteau Words, page 54.

tyre fryer
A boy racer who revs his car up for maximum wheelspin before driving off.

See also Modern Rhyming Terms, page 45.

U

über
The German word for 'over' or 'above', though in *Blinglish* it is now used to intensify an insult, as with 'übernerd', 'überminger' and 'überchav'.

See also *alpha*.

ug
An ugly person, a *minger*. As in:

'Trinny and Susannah can't talk. They're right ugs.'

See also *biffa*, *fugly*, *gipper*, *gonk*, *minger*, *munter*, *swamp donkey*, *wouldn't touch her with yours*.

unbling

Anything that does, or is, the opposite of *bling*, like a pendant from Argos.

under manners

If someone is under manners to you, they have admitted to being weak and inferior, and have agreed to be your personal slave. If they disobey you in any way, you should shout 'manners!' and *hand out some slaps*.

unsafe

Anything that fails to meet the approval of a *kev*, like *moshers*, *grebs* and *freaks*.

See also *blows*, *budget*, *lame*, *sucks*, *wack*, *weary*.

us

Blinglish for 'me', which is itself *Blinglish* for 'my'. As in:

'Could you pass us me *moby*, please?'

uzi

An Israeli-built sub-machine gun. What you threaten to pull on someone if they make eye contact with you in the kebab shop at 2 a.m.

V

vexed

To be annoyed. As in:

'All I said was that you've put on weight. I don't know what you're getting so vexed about.'

See also *aggie*, *flexing*.

village

Your local area, synonymous with being small, provincial or useless. As in:

'I'm not going to Monroe's. It's *well* village.'

See also *ends*, *manor*, *round our way*.

VTS

A visible thong strap, which is the modern equivalent of visible panty line. The ultimate *kappa slappa* and *chavette* fashion statement; brazenly displaying a thong strap that can be separated from the top of a pair of low-slung jeans by anything up to 10 inches of arse.

W

wack

Anything rubbish, or bad, in the old-fashioned sense of the word.

See also *blows*, *budget*, *lame*, *sucks*, *unsafe*, *weary*.

. . . wad

A suffix that can be added to the end of any insult to make it sound more American and therefore cooler, if you're thirteen years old. For example, 'dickwad', 'dorkwad' and 'gaywad'.

wa gwan?

Contraction of 'what's going on?', which is a West Indian-derived greeting.

wanksta

A US term for someone pretending to be a *gangsta*. It's a contraction of 'wack gangsta' rather than a five-knuckle-shuffle reference – they don't even have the word 'wank' over there. Or 'bollocks', for that matter.

wanky

Anything (or anyone) arty or pretentious. As in:

Bloke: Who are all those wanky fuckers?

Girl: Tom Paulin, Germaine Greer and Mark Lawson, actually.

was all like

US slang for 'said'. As in:

'So she was all like, "you're such a slut", and I was all like, "whatever".'

wasted

To be drunk.

See also *lashed, leathered, mullered, munted, ratarsed, ripped*.

waster

Someone who is permanently drunk. Sounds a bit cooler than 'alcoholic'.

See also *caner*.

watless

Something or someone useless. Derived from 'worthless', spoken in a West Indian accent. As in:

'Get out of my house, you watless piece of shit.'

weary

A Northern word used to describe anything rubbish or boring. As in:

'Do we have to go to bingo again, Mum? It's weary.'

See also *blows, budget, lame, sucks, unsafe, wack*.

well

Blinglish for 'very'. As in:

'That Donnay T-shirt looks well *mint*.'

See also *dead, proper, pure*.

westside / eastside

Originally referred to the East and West coasts of America. Now used by *wankstas* everywhere from Watford to Newport to refer to the side of town they come from.

what

Blinglish for 'that'. As in:

'Jason, have you got that five pound what I *borrowed* you?'

whatever

A generic reply to insults that ranks at the bottom of the comeback hierarchy. Used primarily when someone can't think of a comeback in an argument, but doesn't want to keep quiet and lose face. Can be used with a corresponding hand

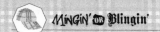

gesture, which is created by making a 'W' shape with your thumbs and index fingers.

See also Comeback Hierarchy, page 147, Modern Sign Language, page 78.

what the dilly-o?

An enquiry, taken from 'what's the deal, yo?'

See also *skinny, 411.*

wheels

Your vehicle. As in:

'I've just got some *proper* fucking speakers fitted in my wheels.'

white man's overbite

The face pulled by *disco vicars* when trying to be cool, which involves biting down on the bottom lip in a look of constipated concentration. The look on David Brent's face when he dances in *The Office* is probably the most famous example of this.

Comeback Hierarchy	
SAMPLE INSULT: 'YOU'RE A BITCH.'	
Sophistication of comeback	Sample comebacks
↑	'I know I am. It stands for "Babe In Total Control of Herself".'
	'Your mum's a bitch.'
	'I know you are.'
	'Talk to the hand.'
	'Bothered.'
	'Whatever.'

whitey

- A white person.

- A description of the reaction of a first-timer or lightweight to cannabis, where the skin pales due to a decrease in blood pressure. As in:

'Oh shit, Wayne's pulled a whitey. Who's gonna drive us home now?'

wife beater

An affectionate term for Stella Artois lager that stands somewhat at odds with its classy *Jean de Florette* marketing image. Derives from the behaviour of someone (normally a *townie*) after having consumed a skinful.

wifey

A girlfriend you have actual feelings about, rather than just a *ride* or a *fuckbuddy*. Can be used by *playas* to denote the favourite of their many women.

See also *boo*.

wigga

A white youth who aspires to the *gangsta* lifestyle – most of them these days.

wingman

Someone who enables you to pull the girl you fancy by getting off with her *fugly* friend. The opposite of a *cock blocker*.

See also *take one for the team*.

wiv

Blinglish for 'with'. As in:

Townie 1: Who did you go down *maccy ds* wiv?

Townie 2: Me mum and her boyfriend.

wouldn't touch her with yours

The appropriate thing to say when commenting on an ugly woman, or a girl with a *nice personality*.

See also *biffa, fugly, gipper, gonk, minger, munter, swamp donkey, ug*.

Y

yall

Southern US contraction of 'you all' that has made its way
into youth slang via hip-hop music. As in:

'Yall can *fuck off* if you think you're having any of my Fruit Pastilles.'

yard

West Indian term for home. Can be used to mean your actual
house as well as your home country, which is where
'yardie' originates.

yates's

Yates's Wine Lodge. A ubiquitous chain of bars, and the best
place to go if you want to cop off with the local *skanks*,
townies and *chavettes*.

yayo

Cocaine. Derived from the term 'llello' as used by Tony
Montana in *Scarface*.

yo
Popular US-derived term used for getting someone's attention. As in:

'Yo! If I give you this three pound, will you go in there and buy *us* ten fags?'

yoos
The *Blinglish* plural of 'you'. As in:

'I'm getting a large chips and yoos aren't having none.'

you the man
An expression of approval.

See also *no, you the man*.

yout
Wanky **word to refer to young people. '*Da* yout' recently replaced 'ver kids' and 'the yoof' as the way to refer to young people by media types.**

you wish

What to say when pretending to offer a crisp to a *pikey* before drawing the packet away at the last minute.

Z

z

The letter that replaces 's' to make a plural in *Blinglish*. For example, 'bitchez', 'gangstaz' and 'sad twatz'.

z-list

The bottom rung of celebrities, the shitterati, and the crap pack. Includes reality-TV stars, obscure boy-band members and ex-celebrities who have turned into tragic parodies of themselves.

101

Derived from the US practice of naming elementary courses at universities, it means an introduction to something, or the basics. As in:

'Looks like someone needs Asswhooping 101.'

187

Slang for murder. From the US police code for a homicide. As in:

'Tell Brandon to give me my ruler back, or I'll 187 him.'

411

Information, or the low-down on something, derived from the telephone Directory Enquiries number in the US.

See also *skinny, what the dilly-o?*

404

A clueless person. From the web message '404 not found', which appears when your internet browser could not locate

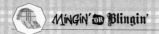

the page you were looking for, and continuing the tradition of 'the lights are on, but nobody's home'.

Voguish Words

Trendy terms that have entered modern English, and those that you'll come across reading the Sunday papers.

blog
An online diary, or 'web log'. As in:
'This movie *blows*. I think I'll *diss* it on my blog.'

egosurfing
Looking for references to yourself on the web. Usually results in printing off a picture of a bald American businessman with the same name as you and showing it to everyone in your office.

flashmob
A large group of people who receive a text message or web instruction, and gather in a public place to do something simultaneously.

googling

Searching for someone else's name on the web, especially before going out on a date with them.

guilty pleasure

Something you like in spite of yourself, like WWF, McFly and *Dick and Dom in Da Bungalow*.

hand-me-up

An item such as a computer or MP3 player, that a young person gives to an older person because they've bought a better one to replace it.

jump the shark

Something 'jumps the shark' if it suddenly declines in quality after being consistently good. From an episode of *Happy Days* where the Fonz waterskis over a shark.

studentification

The changes caused to an area of a town by large numbers of students moving in, such as more all-night garages, arthouse cinemas and ethnic hat shops.

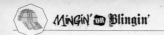
New Blinglish Words